D1015047

the pressure cooker cookbook

with
Debra Murray

Copyright © 2010 Debra Murray

All rights reserved. No portion of this book may be reproduced, stored in a retrieval system, or transmitted in any form by any means, mechanical, electronic, photocopying, recording or otherwise, without written permission from the publisher.

www.cookbookdesigner.com

Printed in the U.S.A.

I am so blessed to be able to create and share this cookbook. It is the culmination of so many talented and supportive people:

First, I would like to thank my incredible family. My beloved husband Martin, my bright and beautiful daughter Nevar, my incredible parents Yvette and Reggie, my devoted sister Gail as well as my darling step grand children Brennan and Patrick. Your love and encouragement is the fuel that drives everything I do.

I would like to thank Wolfgang Puck, my incredible boss, friend and mentor. You not only taught me how to cook, but how to live, love and laugh. Thank you for allowing me to publish these cookbooks. It is a dream come true for me and I treasure the 12 years we have worked together.

Thank you to Sydney Silverman for running this remarkable company and for your commitment to service and quality. Mike Sanseverino, bless you for engineering this brilliant pressure cooker. It is literally going to change the world for the better.

Thank you to Jonathan Schwartz and Daniel Koren. These books are the outcome of your talents and hard work. Thank you for all you do.

Thank you to Marian Getz, who not only works so hard to bring all of our cooking shows to life, but teaches me many hidden cooking secrets that no one has ever published. I am so grateful for every minute we spend together.

Thank you to Chris Davis, my brilliant photographer. I cherish every second we work together. Your goodness is so inspiring.

Thank you to Tracy Ferguson, my talented food stylist as well as Cameron Fritz for your hard work.

Thanks to everyone who reaches out to me by email, the rice cooker group or the pressure cooker group. I would also like to thank the people from my church.

Most of all I want to thank the kind HSN viewers who purchase our products and books. It is all your love and support that deserves the biggest thank you. God Bless you all.

pressure cooker is surrounded by
ies ranging from lids flying off to soup
pping from the ceiling. While older
ssure cookers may have caused these
sodes, today's generation of pressure
kers are modified to ensure safe and
y cooking. This appliance is designed
use steam pressure to break down
fibers of the food, allowing for faster
king times. Tough meats become
der quickly, vegetables and grains are
used with flavors and foods retain their
rients. Although the pressure cooker
mainly used as a timesaving device, it
rks for fine cooking as well.

ora Murray has been my assistant at
Home Shopping Network for over
years, and I know her passion for
lity appliances that can make anyone
etter cook. Debra knows how to use
pressure cooker in remarkable ways.
passion for cooking and experimental
ure created this amazing collection of
ipes. I have urged her to share them
h as many people as possible through
book.

extremely talented cook, Debra shares
WELL (Wolfgang's Eat, Love, Live!™)
losophy of good cooking and warm
spitality. I believe everyone should
the freshest, all-natural ingredients,
ally grown, organic when possible,
raised using sustainable humane
thods.

arned long ago, beside my mother and
ndmother, one should always put lots
ove into cooking. This is evident in this
ok of Debra Murray's pressure cooker
ipes.

table of contents

acknowledgements   2
introduction by wolfgang puck   3
pressure cooker tips   6
index   142

soups & stews   8

fresh vegetable soup   9
tomato florentine   10
kabocha squash soup   12
hot sour noodle soup with shrimp   14
shrimp bisque   16
martin's lobster asparagus soup   18
potato leek soup   20
pizza soup   22
lentils with italian turkey sausage   24
low country boil   26
rich chicken stock   28
chicken soup   30
greek lemon chicken soup   32
chicken & dumpling soup   34
swiss chard white bean stew   36
pork & apple stew   38
rich beef stock   40
classic beef stew   42
beef bourguignon   44

grains & pasta   46

steel cut oats   47
wheat berry salad   48
creamy spinach mashed potatoes   50
wild rice with dried cranberries & pecan stuffing   52
spicy bulgur pilaf   54
creamy quinoa pudding   56
quinoa turkey meatloaf   58
stuffed turkey peppers with couscous   60
buffalo chicken mac & cheese   62
reisfleisch   64

vegetables   66

artichokes in lemon dill   67
baby beets & carrots   68
beet greens with smoked turkey wings   70
lemon dill green beans   72
brussels sprouts with pearl onions   74

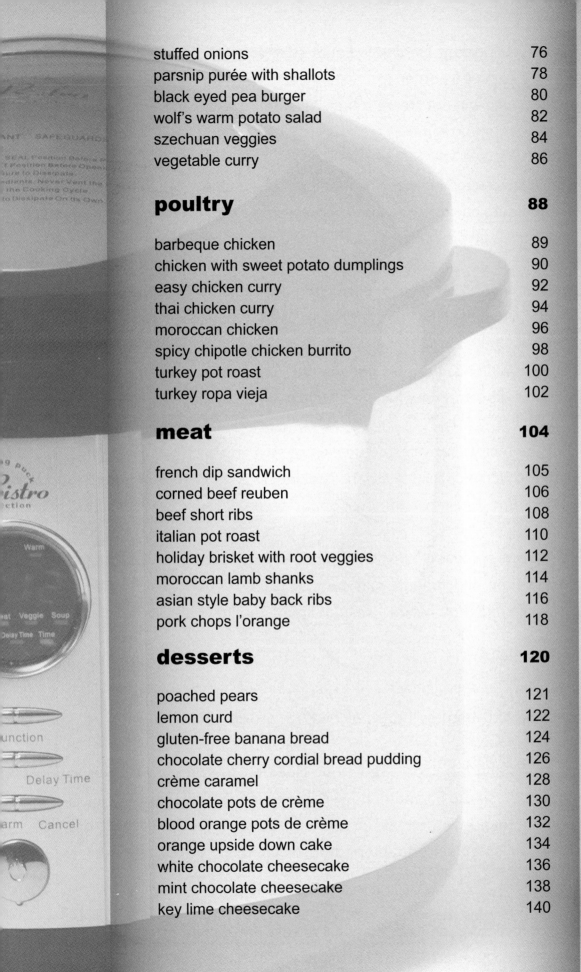

stuffed onions 76
parsnip purée with shallots 78
black eyed pea burger 80
wolf's warm potato salad 82
szechuan veggies 84
vegetable curry 86

poultry 88

barbeque chicken 89
chicken with sweet potato dumplings 90
easy chicken curry 92
thai chicken curry 94
moroccan chicken 96
spicy chipotle chicken burrito 98
turkey pot roast 100
turkey ropa vieja 102

meat 104

french dip sandwich 105
corned beef reuben 106
beef short ribs 108
italian pot roast 110
holiday brisket with root veggies 112
moroccan lamb shanks 114
asian style baby back ribs 116
pork chops l'orange 118

desserts 120

poached pears 121
lemon curd 122
gluten-free banana bread 124
chocolate cherry cordial bread pudding 126
crème caramel 128
chocolate pots de crème 130
blood orange pots de crème 132
orange upside down cake 134
white chocolate cheesecake 136
mint chocolate cheesecake 138
key lime cheesecake 140

pressure cooker tips

- It is very important to have a liquid such as water, stock, juice or wine in the pressure cooker in order to create steam. Thicker liquids such as barbecue or tomato sauce will not create steam. At least 1 to 2 cups of liquid are necessary to create adequate steam.

- When converting these recipes for pressure cookers other than the Wolfgang Puck pressure cooker, use your low pressure setting for recipes using the VEGGIE function. For all other recipes in this book, use your high pressure setting.

- When cooking a rice, bean or pasta dish, do not fill the pressure cooker more than halfway. When cooking soups or stocks, do not exceed the ²/₃ mark.

- If you live in higher altitudes, you may increase the cooking time slightly. I suggest adding 5% cooking time for every 1000 feet above sea level.

- All of the recipes were tested by weight so if you wish to cook a larger piece of meat, you will need to increase the cooking time. Add 10 minutes to the suggested cooking time for every additional pound of meat.

- Every piece of meat is not graded or marbled with the same amount of fat and cooking time adjustments may be necessary. If your meat is not as tender as you would like, simply add ½ cup of liquid and increase the cooking time by 10 minutes.

- Here are some guidelines for rice that work for me: On the RICE function, white rice cooks in 6 minutes, brown or wild rice cooks in 20 minutes.

- The valves and regulator need to be clean for the pressure cooker to function properly. Wash the lid and remove the regulator for cleaning. The gasket should always be hand washed and properly fitted back on the lid as it prevents the steam from escaping. If not properly installed, steam will escape under the lid and pressure will not be achieved.

- I do not recommend using the quick release method for letting the pressure out. I have timed the recipes in this book with the pressure going out on its own. Remember to never attempt to open the lid while pressure cooking is in progress.

If you every complete a recipe and the cooking liquid is thinner than you desire, simply press the RICE function and let the liquid reduce with the lid off until the desired consistency is achieved.

Please use the chart below for your reference:

INGREDIENT	AMOUNT	FUNCTION	TIME (Minutes)	LIQUID SUGGESTED (Cups)
VEGETABLES				
Artichokes, trimmed	3 med	Veggie	14	2
Beans, Black	1 cup	Veggie	12	2
Beans, Navy	1 cup	Veggie	8	2 - 2 1/2
Beans, Pinto	1 cup	Rice	15	3
Beans, Red Kidney	1 cup	Rice	20	3 1/2
Beans, String	1 lb	Veggie	3	1
Beets	6 med	Veggie	15	2
Cabbage head, quartered	1 med	Veggie	10	2
Carrots 2" pieces	2 cups	Veggie	5	1
Corn on the cob	6 ears	Veggie	4	1 1/2
Parsnips, cubed	2 cups	Veggie	4	1 1/2
Squash , Acorn, halved	4 halves	Veggie	13	2
Squash, Butternut, 1/2" slices	8 slices	Veggie	4	1 1/2
MEATS, POULTRY, SEAFOOD				
Beef Brisket	3 lbs	Meat	90	2-3
Beef Ribs	6 whole	Meat	30	2
Chicken, boneless, skinless pieces, frozen	4 lbs	Meat	5	2
Chicken, legs	4 whole	Meat	20	2
Chicken, quartered	1 whole	Meat	20	2
Chicken, whole	3 lbs	Meat	20	3
Chuck Roast	3 lbs	Meat	75	2-3
Corned Beef	3 lbs	Meat	90	3
Baby Back Ribs	2 slabs	Meat	20	2
Lamb Shanks	2-3 lbs	Meat	30	2
Pork Chops (8-10 oz each)	3-4	Meat	12	2
Pork Loin	2 lbs	Meat	22	3
Short Ribs	3 lbs	Meat	35	2
Spare Ribs	1 slab	Meat	30	2
Stew Meat 1" pieces	3 lbs	Meat	18	4
Turkey Breast	5 lbs	Meat	45	3
Veal Shanks (8 oz each)	3	Meat	30	2
POTATOES				
Potato, Baking	4 large	Veggie	15	2
Potatoes, Red Bliss (2 oz each)	up to 20	Veggie	7	2
Potatoes, White, cubed	3 cups	Veggie	5	1 1/2

soups & stews

fresh vegetable soup

1. Place all ingredients into the pressure cooker; secure lid.

2. Set pressure cooker to SOUP and timer to 10 minutes.

3. When cooking is complete, remove thyme sprig and serve.

makes 6 servings

INGREDIENTS

½ cup sweet onions, diced
3 garlic cloves, sliced
¼ cup celery, diced
¼ cup carrots, peeled and sliced
¼ cup celery root, peeled and diced
¼ cup green beans, cut into ½-inch pieces
¼ cup fresh corn kernels
¼ cup Brussels sprouts, diced
1 can (14.5 ounces) petite diced tomatoes
3 cups beef stock
1 teaspoon sea salt
1 teaspoon freshly ground pepper
1 sprig fresh thyme

tomato florentine

1. Place all ingredients, except basil, into the pressure cooker; secure lid.

2. Set pressure cooker to SOUP and timer to 8 minutes.

3. When cooking is complete, top with basil and serve.

(*Deb's Tip:*
Garnish with a touch of pesto.)

makes 4 to 6 servings

INGREDIENTS

2 pounds grape tomatoes
6 cups chicken stock
1 medium onion, chopped
1 carrot, peeled and sliced
3 garlic cloves, sliced
1 teaspoon salt
1 teaspoon freshly ground pepper
1 cup dry pasta
1 cup baby spinach leaves
5 basil leaves, torn

kabocha squash soup

1. Place all ingredients into the pressure cooker; secure lid.

2. Set pressure cooker to SOUP and timer to 10 minutes.

3. When cooking is complete, purée the soup using an immersion blender until desired consistency and serve.

Deb's Tip:
Garnish with sour cream and cranberry sauce.

makes 4 to 6 servings

INGREDIENTS

1 (2.5 pound) kabocha squash, peeled, seeded and cut into 2-inch pieces
1 small onion, chopped
2 tablespoons ginger, sliced
3 garlic cloves
1 teaspoon salt
1 teaspoon freshly ground pepper
2 cups chicken stock
¼ cup orange juice
1 tablespoon brown sugar

hot sour noodle soup with shrimp

1. Place all ingredients, except rice noodles, into the pressure cooker; secure lid.

2. Set pressure cooker to SOUP and timer to 10 minutes.

3. When cooking is complete, remove the lemongrass then add the rice noodles to the pressure cooker; stir.

4. Divide the soup between bowls and serve.

makes 4 to 6 servings

INGREDIENTS

5 cups chicken stock
4 garlic cloves, sliced
1 tablespoon fresh ginger, grated
1 star anise
3 tablespoons fish sauce
1 tablespoon soy sauce
1 teaspoon brown sugar
1 Serrano chili pepper, seeds and membrane removed, thinly sliced

1 lemongrass stalk, halved
1 teaspoon lime zest
1 tablespoon lime juice
1 pound shrimp, peeled and deveined
2 cups bean sprouts
2 green onions, cut into 1-inch pieces
2 tablespoons cilantro leaves, chopped
2 tablespoons fresh mint leaves, chopped
6 ounces rice noodles, cooked

shrimp bisque

1. Dry the shrimp using paper towels.

2. Preheat the oil in a sauté pan over medium-high heat.

3. Add the shrimp to the pan and cook for 3 minutes on each side.

4. Season the shrimp with salt, pepper and paprika then transfer them to the pressure cooker.

5. Add the wine to the pan; scrape up all the little bits from the bottom of the pan then transfer the pan contents to the pressure cooker.

6. Add remaining ingredients, except heavy cream, to the pressure cooker; secure lid.

7. Set pressure cooker to SOUP and timer to 6 minutes.

8. When cooking is complete, remove the tarragon sprig.

9. Using an immersion blender, purée the soup while adding the cream; purée until desired consistency before serving.

makes 4 to 6 servings

INGREDIENTS

2 pounds large shrimp, with shells
2 tablespoons extra-virgin olive oil
1 teaspoon salt
1 teaspoon freshly ground pepper
1 teaspoon sweet paprika
1 cup white wine
1 carrot, peeled and chopped
1 celery stalk, chopped

1 leek (white part only), sliced
1 garlic clove, sliced
1 small potato, peeled and halved
1 tablespoon tomato paste
3 cups chicken stock
1 sprig tarragon
2 teaspoons sherry
1 cup heavy cream

martin's lobster asparagus soup

1. Place all ingredients, except cream cheese, into the pressure cooker; secure lid.

2. Set pressure cooker to SOUP and timer to 10 minutes.

3. When cooking is complete, remove the lobster meat from the tails and discard the shells.

4. Cut the lobster meat into 1/2-inch pieces and place them back into the pressure cooker.

5. Add the cream cheese to the pressure cooker and stir until dissolved.

6. Serve hot or cold.

makes 4 servings

INGREDIENTS

2 cups chicken stock
1 cup white wine
1 lemon, halved
1 leek (white part only), sliced
1 celery stalk
2 lobster tails, with shells
1 teaspoon lemon pepper seasoning
1 pound fresh asparagus, cut into 1-inch pieces
4 ounces cream cheese

potato leek soup

1. Place all ingredients, except sour cream and chives, into the pressure cooker; secure lid.

2. Set pressure cooker to SOUP and timer to 10 minutes.

3. When cooking is complete, purée the soup using an immersion blender until desired consistency is achieved.

4. Serve topped with sour cream and chives.

Deb's Tip:
This soup is even more delicious served cold.

makes 4 to 6 servings

INGREDIENTS

2 cups leeks (white part only), sliced
1 cup sweet onions, sliced
2 cups Yukon Gold potatoes, peeled and diced
3 cups chicken stock
½ teaspoon salt
½ teaspoon freshly ground pepper
½ cup sour cream
1 teaspoon fresh chives, chopped

pizza soup

1. Place all ingredients, except mozzarella cheese, into the pressure cooker; secure lid.

2. Set pressure cooker to SOUP and timer to 8 minutes.

3. When cooking is complete, divide the soup between bowls, top with cheese and serve.

Deb's Tip:
Serve with a piece of garlic bread on the side.

makes 4 to 6 servings

INGREDIENTS

1 can (28 ounces) petite diced tomatoes
1 medium onion, chopped
4 garlic cloves, sliced
4 cups chicken stock
1 teaspoon salt
1 teaspoon freshly ground pepper
1 teaspoon dried oregano
1 pound Italian turkey sausage, thinly sliced
3 ounces turkey pepperoni, diced
1 green bell pepper, diced
½ cup dry ditalini pasta
½ cup mozzarella cheese, shredded

lentils with italian turkey sausage

1. Place all ingredients into the pressure cooker; stir then secure the lid.

2. Set pressure cooker to MEAT and timer to 20 minutes.

3. When cooking is complete, discard the bay leaf and serve.

makes 4 servings

INGREDIENTS

1 pound sweet Italian turkey sausage, cut into 1-inch pieces
1 medium onion, diced
2 garlic cloves, sliced
1 large carrot, peeled and thinly sliced
1 celery stalk, thinly sliced
1 cup lentils
2 cups chicken stock
1 can (14.5 ounces) diced tomatoes with garlic and olive oil
1 bay leaf
½ teaspoon crushed red pepper flakes (optional)

low country boil

1. Place all ingredients, except corn, shrimp and clams, into the pressure cooker; secure lid.

2. Set pressure cooker to VEGGIE and timer to 10 minutes.

3. When cooking is complete, add remaining ingredients to the pressure cooker; secure lid.

4. Set pressure cooker to VEGGIE and timer to 5 minutes.

5. When cooking is complete, serve immediately.

Deb's Tip:
I like to place my pressure cooker in the middle of the table, have bibs for all my guests and serve with drawn butter.

makes 4 to 6 servings

INGREDIENTS

5 cups water
1 cup white wine
1 medium onion, quartered
4 whole garlic cloves
1 lemon, halved
1 tablespoon kosher salt
1 teaspoon cayenne pepper
1 celery stalk
1 tablespoon pickling spice
1 tablespoon crab seasoning
6 red bliss potatoes
1 pound spicy smoked sausage
2 ears of corn, cut in half
2 pounds large shrimp, in the shell
1 dozen little neck clams, cleaned and in the shell

rich chicken stock

1. Preheat oven to 350 degrees.

2. Place the chicken wings in a large oven-proof skillet.

3. Add the oil, salt, pepper and poultry seasoning to the skillet; toss.

4. Add leek, parsnip and garlic to the skillet; toss again.

5. Place the skillet in the oven and roast for 1 hour.

6. Transfer the skillet contents to the pressure cooker.

7. Add the wine to deglaze the skillet; scrape up all the little bits from the bottom of the pan and pour it into the pressure cooker.

8. Add remaining ingredients to the pressure cooker; secure lid.

9. Set pressure cooker to MEAT and timer to 30 minutes.

10. When cooking is complete, strain the stock through a fine sieve into a container with a lid.

11. Refrigerate the stock covered for 3 hours.

12. Remove hardened fat from the top of the stock.

13. Stock will keep refrigerated for up to one week or frozen for up to 6 months.

makes 4 cups

INGREDIENTS

2 pounds whole chicken wings, raw
1 tablespoon extra-virgin olive oil
1 tablespoon sea salt
1 teaspoon black pepper
1 teaspoon poultry seasoning
1 leek (white part only), split
1 parsnip, peeled, cut into 1-inch pieces

3 garlic cloves
1 cup white wine
3 cups water
2 celery stalks, cut into 2-inch pieces
1 teaspoon turmeric powder
2 sprigs fresh thyme

chicken soup

1. Place all ingredients, except celery, carrots, noodles and parsley, into the pressure cooker; secure lid.

2. Set pressure cooker to SOUP and timer to 30 minutes.

3. When cooking is complete, strain the pressure cooker contents through a sieve into a container.

4. Refrigerate the stock for 30 minutes.

5. Remove the chicken meat from the bones, place the meat back into the pressure cooker and discard the bones.

6. Remove the stock from the refrigerator, discard the hardened fat from the top then pour it back into the pressure cooker.

7. Add remaining ingredients to the pressure cooker; secure lid.

8. Set pressure cooker to SOUP and timer to 5 minutes.

9. When cooking is complete, serve immediately.

makes 6 servings

INGREDIENTS

1 (5 pound) whole chicken
4 cups water
2 teaspoons sea salt
1 teaspoon turmeric powder
½ teaspoon black pepper
1 sprig fresh thyme
1 leek (white part only), halved
2 garlic cloves
2 celery stalks, cut into 2-inch pieces
2 whole carrots, peeled and cut into 2-inch pieces
½ cup dry egg noodles
1 tablespoon flat leaf parsley, chopped

greek lemon chicken soup

1. Place all ingredients, except quinoa, lemon juice, eggs and mint leaves, into the pressure cooker; secure lid.

2. Set pressure cooker to MEAT and timer to 20 minutes.

3. When cooking is complete, pour the pressure cooker contents through a strainer, separating the stock from the chicken and vegetables.

4. Pour the stock into the pressure cooker.

5. Discard all vegetables and chop the chicken; set aside.

6. Add the quinoa to the pressure cooker.

7. Set pressure cooker to RICE and timer to 5 minutes; cook with the lid off.

8. When cooking is complete, combine the lemon juice, eggs and yolk in a bowl; whisk well.

9. Ladle 1/4 cup of hot stock into the egg mixture; whisk well.

10. Drizzle the egg mixture into the pressure cooker while continuously whisking.

11. Add the chicken and mint to the pressure cooker.

12. Cook for an additional 3 minutes before serving.

makes 6 servings

INGREDIENTS

6 cups chicken stock
2 boneless, skinless chicken breasts
1 teaspoon salt
1 teaspoon freshly ground pepper
½ teaspoon turmeric powder
1 bay leaf
1 teaspoon lemon zest
1 medium onion, chopped

1 celery stalk, sliced
1 carrot, peeled and sliced
¼ cup quinoa, rinsed
½ cup lemon juice
2 large eggs, beaten
1 egg yolk, beaten
2 tablespoons mint leaves, chopped

chicken & dumpling soup

1. Cut the chicken into 1-inch pieces and pat dry using paper towels.

2. Preheat the oil in a large sauté pan over medium-high heat.

3. Place the chicken into the pan.

4. Season the chicken with salt, pepper and poultry seasoning; brown the chicken on each side then transfer to the pressure cooker.

5. Add the wine to deglaze the pan; scrape up all the little bits from the bottom of the pan then transfer the pan contents to the pressure cooker.

6. Add remaining soup ingredients to the pressure cooker; secure lid.

7. Set pressure cooker to SOUP and timer to 10 minutes.

8. While the soup is cooking, combine all dumpling ingredients in a bowl; do not overmix.

9. When cooking is complete, discard the thyme sprig.

10. With the lid off, set pressure cooker to RICE; when the soup simmers, drop small dumplings into the soup using a teaspoon until all the batter has been used.

11. Carefully turn the dumplings using a teaspoon, cook through and serve.

makes 6 servings

SOUP INGREDIENTS	DUMPLING INGREDIENTS
4 boneless, skinless chicken breasts	1¼ cups unbleached all purpose flour
2 tablespoons extra-virgin olive oil	2 teaspoons baking powder
1 teaspoon salt	½ teaspoon salt
½ teaspoon freshly ground pepper	¼ teaspoon freshly ground pepper
1 teaspoon poultry seasoning	1 large egg, beaten
½ cup white wine	1 tablespoon butter, melted
5 cups chicken stock	½ cup half & half
2 celery stalks, cut into 1-inch pieces	1 teaspoon dried parsley
2 carrots, peeled and cut into 1-inch slices	
1 leek (white part only), thinly sliced	
2 garlic cloves, sliced	
1 sprig fresh thyme	

swiss chard
white bean stew

1. Place all the ingredients into the pressure cooker; secure lid.

2. Set pressure cooker to VEGGIE and timer to 10 minutes.

3. When cooking is complete, remove the thyme sprigs and serve.

(*Deb's Tip:*
Serve this delicious stew topped with grated Parmesan cheese and a slice of crusty bread.)

makes 4 to 6 servings

INGREDIENTS

1 bunch Swiss chard, washed and cut into 1-inch pieces
1 medium sweet onion, diced
3 garlic cloves, sliced
1 pound red bliss potatoes, washed and diced
1 cup white beans, cooked
2 sprigs fresh thyme
1 cup vegetable stock
1 teaspoon salt
½ teaspoon freshly ground pepper

37

pork & apple stew

1. Preheat oil in a large skillet over medium-high heat.

2. Season the pork with salt, pepper, fennel and rosemary.

3. Add the pork to the skillet and sear for 2 minutes on each side.

4. Transfer the pork to the pressure cooker.

5. Add the chicken stock to deglaze the skillet; scrape up all the little bits from the bottom of the skillet then transfer the skillet contents to the pressure cooker.

6. Add half of the apples to the pressure cooker; secure lid.

7. Set pressure cooker to STEW and timer to 30 minutes.

8. When cooking is complete add cabbage, potatoes and remaining apples to the pressure cooker; secure lid.

9. Set pressure cooker to VEGGIE and timer to 5 minutes.

10. When cooking is complete, serve immediately.

Deb's Tip:
Serve with a touch of cider vinegar.

makes 4 servings

INGREDIENTS

2 tablespoons extra-virgin olive oil
1 pork loin roast (1½ pounds), cut into 2-inch chunks
1 teaspoon salt
1 teaspoon freshly ground pepper
½ teaspoon fennel seeds
1 teaspoon rosemary leaves
1 cup chicken stock
2 Granny Smith apples, peeled, cored, sliced and divided
1 cup purple cabbage, shredded
6 red bliss potatoes, washed and halved

rich beef stock

1. Preheat oven to 350 degrees.

2. Place the rib bones into an oven-safe skillet.

3. Add the oil, salt and pepper to the skillet; toss.

4. Add the onions, mushrooms and garlic to the skillet; toss again.

5. Place the skillet in the oven and roast for 1 hour.

6. Transfer the skillet contents to the pressure cooker.

7. Add the wine to deglaze the skillet; scrape up all the little bits from the bottom of the skillet then transfer the skillet contents to the pressure cooker.

8. Add remaining ingredients to the pressure cooker; secure lid.

9. Set pressure cooker to MEAT and timer to 45 minutes.

10. When cooking is complete, strain the stock through a fine sieve into a container with a lid.

11. Refrigerate the stock covered for 3 hours.

12. Remove hardened fat from the top of the stock before using.

13. Stock will keep refrigerated for up to one week or frozen for up to 6 months.

makes 4 cups

INGREDIENTS

4 pounds beef rib bones
1 tablespoon extra-virgin olive oil
1 tablespoon sea salt
1 teaspoon freshly ground pepper
4 ounces button mushrooms
1 medium sweet onion, quartered
5 garlic cloves

1 cup red wine
5 cups water
2 celery stalks
1 carrot, peeled
2 sprigs fresh thyme
2 tablespoons tomato paste

classic beef stew

1. Place the beef, salt, pepper, thyme, onions, garlic, stock and wine into the pressure cooker; secure lid.

2. Set pressure cooker to STEW and timer to 20 minutes.

3. When cooking is complete, remove the lid.

4. Add remaining ingredients to the pressure cooker; secure lid.

5. Set pressure cooker to VEGGIE and timer to 5 minutes.

6. When cooking is complete, remove the thyme sprig and serve.

makes 6 to 8 servings

INGREDIENTS

2 pounds lean beef, cut into 1-inch pieces
2 teaspoons sea salt
1 teaspoon freshly ground pepper
1 sprig fresh thyme
1 medium onion, quartered
3 garlic cloves
1 cup beef stock
½ cup port wine
3 large carrots, peeled and cut into 1-inch pieces
8 creamer potatoes, quartered
2 celery stalks, cut into 1-inch pieces
1 parsnip, peeled and diced
3 tablespoons tomato paste
2 tablespoons sweet barbecue sauce

beef bourguignon

1. Preheat oil in a large skillet over medium-high heat.

2. Season the meat with salt and pepper.

3. Place the meat into the skillet; sear each side until browned.

4. Add the mushrooms to the skillet and cook for 3 minutes; stir occasionally.

5. Add the stock to deglaze the skillet; scrape up all the little bits from the bottom of the pan and pour it into the pressure cooker.

6. Add remaining ingredients to the pressure cooker; secure lid.

7. Set pressure cooker to STEW and timer to 30 minutes.

8. When cooking is complete, discard the thyme sprigs and serve.

makes 6 servings

INGREDIENTS

2 tablespoons extra-virgin olive oil
2 pounds chuck roast, cut into ½-inch pieces
1 teaspoon sea salt
½ teaspoon freshly ground pepper
8 ounces baby portobello mushrooms, sliced
1 cup beef stock
1 cup pearl onions
4 garlic cloves
3 sprigs fresh thyme
2 tablespoons black currant jelly
¼ cup crushed tomatoes
2 carrots, peeled and sliced into 2-inch pieces

steel cut oats

1. Place all ingredients into the pressure cooker; secure lid.

2. Set pressure cooker to RICE and timer to 6 minutes.

3. When cooking is complete, remove the cinnamon stick and serve.

makes 4 servings

INGREDIENTS

1 cup steel cut oats
1⅔ cups water
Pinch of salt
1 cinnamon stick
¼ cup soy milk
2 teaspoons agave syrup

wheat berry salad

1. Place the wheat berries, water and salt into the pressure cooker; secure lid.

2. Set pressure cooker to RICE and timer to 35 minutes.

3. When cooking is complete, transfer the wheat berries to a large bowl; let cool to room temperature.

4. Add remaining ingredients to the bowl; toss well.

5. Chill for 30 minutes before serving.

Deb's Tip:
Top with crumbled blue cheese.

makes 6 servings

INGREDIENTS

1 cup wheat berries, rinsed
2 cups water
½ teaspoon salt
1 small sweet onion, chopped
1 English cucumber, seeded and chopped
1 medium tomato, diced
½ teaspoon fresh mint leaves, chopped
1 teaspoon lemon juice
½ teaspoon garlic salt
½ teaspoon freshly ground pepper
2 tablespoons extra-virgin olive oil

49

creamy spinach
mashed potatoes

1. Place all ingredients, except spinach, into the pressure cooker; secure lid.

2. Set pressure cooker to VEGGIE and timer to 8 minutes.

3. When cooking is complete, strain the potatoes; set aside.

4. Place the spinach into the pressure cooker.

5. Set the pressure cooker to RICE and cook with the lid off until the spinach begins to simmer.

6. Add the potatoes to the pressure cooker.

7. Using a potato masher, mash the potatoes to desired consistency, stir and serve.

makes 6 to 8 servings

INGREDIENTS

2 pounds Yukon Gold potatoes, peeled and quartered
1 cup water
1 teaspoon salt
½ teaspoon ground white pepper
1 package (10 ounces) frozen creamed spinach, thawed

wild rice with dried cranberries & pecan stuffing

1. Set pressure cooker to RICE and timer to 40 minutes.

2. Add the turkey to the pressure cooker; cook for 3 minutes with the lid off while breaking up the turkey using a wooden spoon.

3. Add the onions, celery, salt and pepper to the pressure cooker; cook for an additional 2 minutes while continuing to break up the turkey.

4. Add remaining ingredients to the pressure cooker; secure the lid and let cook for the remaining time displayed on the timer.

5. When cooking is complete, stir and serve.

Deb's Tip:
This is the perfect side dish to compliment roast turkey or chicken.

makes 4 to 6 servings

INGREDIENTS

1 pound ground turkey
1 small onion, minced
1 celery stalk, chopped
1 teaspoon salt
½ teaspoon freshly ground pepper
1 teaspoon poultry seasoning
1 cup wild rice, rinsed
3½ cups chicken stock
½ cup dried cranberries
½ cup pecans, chopped
2 sage leaves, chopped

spicy bulgur pilaf

1. Place all ingredients, except cilantro, into the pressure cooker; secure lid.

2. Set pressure cooker to RICE and timer to 6 minutes.

3. When cooking is complete, fluff using a fork, top with cilantro and serve.

Deb's Tip:
Bulgur is a healthy and delicious substitute for rice.

makes 6 servings

INGREDIENTS

1 medium onion, chopped
1 garlic clove, sliced
1 cup bulgur
½ teaspoon turmeric powder
½ teaspoon cumin seeds
1½ cups chicken stock
1 tablespoon lemon zest
½ cup black olives
¼ cup lemon juice
1 tablespoon fresh cilantro leaves, chopped

creamy quinoa pudding

1. Place all ingredients into the pressure cooker; secure lid.

2. Set pressure cooker to RICE and timer to 12 minutes.

3. When cooking is complete, remove the vanilla bean and scrape the inside of the bean into the pudding; stir.

4. Serve immediately.

(*Deb's Tip:*
This pudding is also delicious served chilled.)

makes 4 servings

INGREDIENTS

1 cup quinoa, rinsed
1 cup water
1½ cups rice milk
2 tablespoons agave syrup
Pinch of salt
1 vanilla bean, split
¼ cup dried cherries

quinoa turkey meatloaf

1. In a bowl, combine all ingredients, except tomato sauce and brown sugar; mix well using your hands.

2. Place the meatloaf mixture into the pressure cooker.

3. In a bowl, combine the tomato sauce and brown sugar then pour it over the meatloaf; secure lid.

4. Set pressure cooker to RICE and timer to 20 minutes.

5. When cooking is complete, serve immediately.

makes 4 servings

INGREDIENTS

⅓ cup quinoa, cooked
⅔ cup chicken stock
1 medium onion, chopped
1 sprig tarragon
4 ounces mushrooms, sliced
1 tablespoon Worcestershire sauce
1 pound ground turkey
1 teaspoon salt
½ teaspoon freshly ground pepper
1 large egg, beaten
1 cup tomato sauce
¼ cup brown sugar

stuffed turkey peppers with couscous

1. Set pressure cooker to RICE.

2. Place the turkey into the pressure cooker.

3. With the lid off, cook the turkey for 3 minutes, breaking it up using a wooden spoon.

4. Season the turkey with salt and pepper then add the onions to the pressure cooker and cook for an additional 3 minutes.

5. Add the garlic and saffron to the pressure cooker and cook for an additional 1 minute.

6. Add the tomatoes, couscous and stock to the pressure cooker; stir then secure the lid.

7. Set pressure cooker to RICE and timer to 6 minutes.

8. When cooking is complete, divide the turkey mixture between the peppers.

9. Rinse the pressure cooker insert, place the peppers into the pressure cooker and cover them with tomato sauce; secure lid.

10. Set pressure cooker to RICE and timer to 6 minutes.

11. When cooking is complete, serve immediately.

makes 4 servings

INGREDIENTS

1 pound ground turkey
1 teaspoon salt
1 teaspoon freshly ground pepper
1 medium sweet onion, chopped
3 garlic cloves, minced
4 saffron threads

1 can (14.5 ounces) petite diced tomatoes
½ cup Israeli couscous
1 cup chicken stock
¼ cup Parmesan cheese, grated
4 large bell peppers, membranes removed
1 cup tomato sauce

buffalo chicken mac & cheese

1. Place the chicken, pasta, stock, onions, celery, carrots, wing sauce and ranch seasoning into the pressure cooker; secure lid.

2. Set pressure cook to RICE and timer to 10 minutes.

3. When cooking is complete, add the cream cheese to the pressure cooker; stir until dissolved.

4. Add the cheddar cheese, Swiss cheese and 1/4 cup gorgonzola cheese to the pressure cooker; stir until dissolved.

5. Top with French fried onions and remaining gorgonzola before serving.

makes 4 to 6 servings

INGREDIENTS

6 frozen chicken tenders
3 cups dry rigatoni pasta
3 cups chicken stock
1 small onion, chopped
2 celery stalks, chopped
1 large carrot, peeled and chopped
⅔ cup buffalo wing sauce
1 tablespoon ranch seasoning (optional)
½ cup cream cheese
1 cup sharp cheddar cheese, shredded
1 cup Swiss cheese, shredded
½ cup gorgonzola cheese, crumbled and divided
1 cup cheddar French fried onions, crushed

reisfleisch

1. Set the pressure cooker to RICE.

2. Pour the oil into the pressure cooker and let it preheat with the lid off.

3. Add the onions to the pressure cooker and cook for 2 minutes, stirring occasionally.

4. Add the red peppers and garlic to the pressure cooker; stir.

5. Add the tomato paste to the pressure cooker and cook for an additional 2 minutes.

6. Add remaining ingredients to the pressure cooker; secure lid.

7. Set pressure cooker to RICE and timer to 6 minutes.

8. When cooking is complete, stir and serve immediately.

makes 6 servings

INGREDIENTS

1 tablespoon extra-virgin olive oil
1 medium onion, diced
1 red bell pepper, diced
3 garlic cloves, minced
2 tablespoons tomato paste
1 teaspoon salt
½ teaspoon cayenne pepper
1 teaspoon ground cumin
1 tablespoon Hungarian paprika
½ teaspoon black pepper
1 pound smoked sausage, thinly sliced
½ teaspoon marjoram
2 cups long-grain rice, rinsed
4 cups beef stock

artichokes in lemon dill

1. Place the artichokes, stem-side up, into the pressure cooker.

2. Add remaining ingredients to the pressure cooker; secure lid.

3. Set pressure cooker to VEGGIE and timer to 15 minutes.

4. When cooking is complete, serve hot with some broth on the side.

Deb's Tip:
Chill and serve topped with your favorite vinaigrette dressing.

makes 4 to 6 servings

INGREDIENTS

3 whole artichokes
1 cup white wine
½ cup chicken stock
Juice and zest from 1 lemon
2 sprigs fresh dill
2 garlic cloves

baby beets & carrots

1. Place all ingredients into the pressure cooker; secure lid.

2. Set pressure cooker to VEGGIE and timer to 10 minutes.

3. When cooking is complete, remove the thyme sprig and serve.

makes 4 to 6 servings

INGREDIENTS

1 pound beets, golden and/or red, peeled and quartered
1 pound carrots, yellow and/or orange, peeled and sliced
½ cup rich chicken stock (see recipe on page 28)
½ teaspoon salt
½ teaspoon freshly ground pepper
1 teaspoon lemon zest
1 sprig fresh thyme
2 tablespoons butter

beet greens with smoked turkey wings

1. Place all ingredients, including the turkey wing bone, into the pressure cooker; stir then close the lid.

2. Set pressure cooker to VEGGIE and timer to 10 minutes.

3. When cooking is complete, discard the bone and serve.

Deb's Tip:
Instead of beet tops, you can also use Swiss chard.

makes 4 to 6 servings

INGREDIENTS

3 pounds beet tops, washed and cut into 2-inch pieces
1 smoked turkey wing, meat chopped into ½-inch chunks
1 small sweet onion, chopped
½ cup chicken stock
½ teaspoon salt
½ teaspoon cayenne pepper
Pinch of sugar

71

lemon dill green beans

1. Place all ingredients into the pressure cooker; secure lid.

2. Set pressure cooker to VEGGIE and timer to 5 minutes.

3. When cooking is complete, serve immediately.

makes 6 servings

INGREDIENTS

2 pounds green beans, stems trimmed
¼ cup chicken stock
¼ cup lemon juice
1 teaspoon lemon zest
2 garlic cloves, minced
1 shallot, minced
½ teaspoon salt
½ teaspoon freshly ground pepper
1 tablespoon extra-virgin olive oil
1 teaspoon fresh dill, chopped

brussels sprouts with pearl onions

1. Place all ingredients into the pressure cooker; secure lid.

2. Set pressure cooker to VEGGIE and timer to 8 minutes.

3. When cooking is complete, remove thyme sprig and serve.

Deb's Tip:
I love to serve this with a side of horseradish sauce.

makes 4 servings

INGREDIENTS

1½ pounds Brussels sprouts, trimmed
1 bag (10 ounces) frozen pearl onions
1 cup beef stock
1 teaspoon salt
½ teaspoon freshly ground pepper
1 sprig fresh thyme

stuffed onions

1. Cut the tops and bottoms off the onions then peel off the outer 2 layers.

2. Scoop out the center of each onion until 1 inch is left from the bottom.

3. Preheat the oil in a sauté pan over medium heat.

4. Add the turkey to the pan and brown for 4 minutes while breaking it up using a wooden spoon; season with salt and tarragon while browning.

5. Add the wheat berries, apricots, wine and ½ cup chicken stock to the pan; cook for 6 minutes.

6. Stuff each onion with the mixture then place the onions into the pressure cooker.

7. Pour remaining stock and vinegar into the pressure cooker; secure lid.

8. Set pressure cooker to VEGGIE and timer to 12 minutes.

9. When cooking is complete, serve onions topped with some remaining stock.

makes 4 servings

INGREDIENTS

4 large purple onions
1 tablespoon extra-virgin olive oil
½ pound ground turkey
½ teaspoon salt
½ teaspoon tarragon leaves
2 tablespoons wheat berries
5 apricots, chopped
½ cup white wine
1 cup chicken stock, divided
1 teaspoon white balsamic vinegar

parsnip purée with shallots

1. Place all ingredients, except cream cheese, into the pressure cooker; secure lid.

2. Set pressure cooker to VEGGIE and timer to 7 minutes.

3. When cooking is complete, strain the parsnips then place them into a food processor.

4. Add the cream cheese to the food processor and purée until smooth.

5. Serve immediately.

makes 4 servings

INGREDIENTS

2 pounds parsnips, peeled and cut into 2-inch pieces
1 shallot, minced
⅓ cup chicken stock
½ teaspoon salt
½ teaspoon freshly ground pepper
2 ounces cream cheese

black eyed pea burger

1. Place all ingredients, except flour, bell peppers, salt, pepper and oil, into the pressure cooker; secure lid.

2. Set pressure cooker to VEGGIE and timer to 16 minutes.

3. When cooking is complete, remove the lid and let cool for 30 minutes.

4. Drain the peas and transfer them to a food processor.

5. Add the flour, bell peppers, salt and pepper to the food processor.

6. Process for 30 seconds or until smooth.

7. Take 1/2 cup of the mixture and form it into a patty; repeat with remaining mixture.

8. Preheat the oil in a sauté pan over medium-high heat.

9. Spread additional flour on a plate; roll each patty in the flour.

10. Place the patties into the pan; cook for 2 minutes on each side or until browned.

11. Using a spatula, transfer the patties onto paper towels to drain.

12. Assemble like a burger using your favorite toppings and serve.

makes 4 to 6 servings

INGREDIENTS

8 ounces black eye peas, dried
2½ cups vegetable stock
1 medium sweet onion, chopped
1 celery stalk, sliced
1 carrot, peeled and sliced
1 teaspoon thyme leaves
1 teaspoon salt

½ teaspoon cayenne pepper
1 teaspoon red wine vinegar
2 tablespoons unbleached all purpose flour
1 red bell pepper, seeded and diced
½ teaspoon salt
½ teaspoon freshly ground pepper
¼ cup peanut oil

wolf's warm potato salad

1. Place the potato ingredients into the pressure cooker; secure lid.

2. Set pressure cooker to VEGGIE and timer to 6 minutes.

3. While cooking, combine all marinade ingredients in a bowl; stir.

4. When cooking is complete, strain the potatoes and let them cool for 20 minutes.

5. Slice the potatoes into ¼-inch thick slices then toss them in the marinade.

6. Let potatoes rest for an additional 20 minutes before serving.

makes 4 servings

POTATO INGREDIENTS	MARINADE INGREDIENTS
1 pound fingerling potatoes, washed	1 cup champagne vinegar
3 garlic cloves, sliced	¼ cup peanut oil
3 sprigs fresh parsley	1½ teaspoons kosher salt
2 teaspoons salt	½ teaspoon black pepper
1 cup water	3 tablespoons sugar
	1 tablespoon fresh thyme leaves, chopped
	1 small sweet onion, cut into ¼-inch chunks

szechuan veggies

1. Place all ingredients into the pressure cooker; toss well then secure the lid.

2. Set pressure cooker to VEGGIE and timer to 5 minutes.

3. When cooking is complete, serve immediately.

Deb's Tip:
This is delicious tossed with rice noodles or pasta.

makes 6 servings

INGREDIENTS

3 cups broccoli florets
3 cups cauliflower florets
1 cup carrots, peeled and sliced
1 red bell pepper, julienned
1 medium onion, thinly sliced
1 tablespoon sesame oil
1 tablespoon water
3 tablespoons oyster sauce
1 teaspoon soy sauce
1 tablespoon fresh ginger, grated
2 garlic cloves, minced
1 teaspoon crushed red pepper flakes

vegetable curry

1. Place all ingredients, except cauliflower and carrots, into the pressure cooker; secure lid.

2. Set pressure cooker to VEGGIE and timer to 5 minutes.

3. When cooking is complete, add remaining ingredients to the pressure cooker; secure lid.

4. Set pressure cooker to VEGGIE and timer to 5 minutes.

5. When cooking is complete, serve immediately.

makes 4 servings

INGREDIENTS

1 medium onion, sliced
1 large sweet potato, peeled and diced
1 medium Russet potato, peeled and diced
½ cup chicken stock
1 cup petite diced tomatoes
1 teaspoon ground cumin
1 teaspoon chili powder
2 teaspoons ground coriander
1 teaspoon turmeric powder
1 cup cauliflower florets
½ cup carrots, peeled and sliced

barbeque chicken

1. Place all ingredients into the pressure cooker; secure lid.

2. Set pressure cooker to MEAT and timer to 20 minutes.

3. When cooking is complete, transfer the chicken to a broiler pan, bone-side down.

4. Preheat the broiler on high.

5. To reduce the cooking liquid in the pressure cooker, set to RICE and timer to 10 minutes; let cook with the lid off until the liquid turns into a syrup-like glaze.

6. While the liquid is reducing, place the chicken under the broiler for 7 minutes on each side.

7. Pour barbeque sauce over the chicken and serve with additional sauce on the side.

makes 4 to 6 servings

INGREDIENTS

1 whole chicken fryer, cut into 8 pieces
½ cup chicken stock
1 teaspoon salt
1 teaspoon freshly ground pepper
1 teaspoon dry mustard
1 teaspoon paprika
1 medium onion, diced
3 garlic cloves, minced
2 tablespoons cider vinegar
¼ cup brown sugar
¼ cup ketchup
¼ cup molasses

chicken with sweet potato dumplings

1. Season both sides of the chicken with salt, pepper and rosemary.

2. Preheat the oil in a sauté pan over medium heat.

3. Place the chicken into the pan; brown for 3 minutes on each side.

4. Transfer the chicken to the pressure cooker.

5. Add the wine and stock to the pan; scrape up all the little bits from the bottom of the pan then transfer the pan contents to the pressure cooker.

6. Add remaining chicken ingredients to the pressure cooker; secure lid.

7. Set pressure cooker to MEAT and timer to 25 minutes.

8. While cooking, combine all dumpling ingredients in a bowl; mix well.

9. When cooking is complete, discard the thyme sprig.

10. With the lid off, set pressure cooker to RICE.

11. While simmering, drop dumplings by the spoonful into the pressure cooker.

12. Cook the dumplings for 3 minutes on each side before serving.

makes 6 servings

CHICKEN INGREDIENTS

6 chicken thighs, bone-in, without skin
1 teaspoon salt
1 teaspoon freshly ground pepper
½ teaspoon rosemary leaves, chopped
1 tablespoon extra-virgin olive oil
¼ cup white wine
1 cup chicken stock
½ cup pearl onions
1 celery stalk, sliced
1 large carrot, peeled and sliced
1 sprig fresh thyme
¼ cup tiny frozen peas, thawed

DUMPLING INGREDIENTS

1¼ cups unbleached all purpose flour
1 cup mashed sweet potatoes
½ teaspoon salt
2 teaspoons baking powder
1½ cups buttermilk

easy chicken curry

1. Place all ingredients, except yogurt and cilantro, into the pressure cooker; secure lid.

2. Set pressure cooker to MEAT and timer to 25 minutes.

3. When cooking is complete, transfer the chicken to a platter.

4. Add the yogurt to the stock inside the pressure cooker; stir.

5. Pour mixture over the chicken, top with cilantro and serve.

makes 4 servings

INGREDIENTS

2 pounds skinless chicken legs
1 cup chicken stock
¼ cup brown sugar
1 tablespoon curry powder
1 teaspoon garam masala
1 medium onion, chopped
1 red bell pepper, julienned
1 can (14.5 ounces) petite diced tomatoes
1 cup plain yogurt
1 tablespoon fresh cilantro leaves, chopped

thai chicken curry

1. Place all ingredients, except green onions, into the pressure cooker; secure lid.

2. Set pressure cooker to SOUP and timer to 10 minutes.

3. When cooking is complete, top with green onions and serve.

Deb's Tip:
Serve over hot jasmine rice.

makes 4 to 6 servings

INGREDIENTS

2 cups chicken stock
1 medium onion, diced
3 garlic cloves, sliced
1 tablespoon fresh ginger, sliced
2 tablespoons Thai red curry paste
1 tablespoon lime zest
2 tablespoons fish sauce
2 pounds boneless chicken tenders
2 tablespoons brown sugar
1 red bell pepper, julienned
1 can (13.5 ounces) light coconut milk
1 can (8 ounces) bamboo shoots
2 tablespoons fresh cilantro leaves, chopped
Green onions, chopped

moroccan chicken

1. Using paper towels, pat the chicken dry.

2. Preheat the oil in a sauté pan over medium-high heat.

3. Place the chicken pieces into the pan; season with salt, cumin and nigella seeds.

4. Cook the chicken for 3 minutes on each side or until browned.

5. Transfer the chicken to the pressure cooker.

6. Add the stock to the pan; scrape up all the little bits from the bottom of the pan then transfer the pan contents to the pressure cooker.

7. Add remaining ingredients, except cilantro, to the pressure cooker; secure the lid.

8. Set pressure cooker to MEAT and timer to 20 minutes.

9. When cooking is complete, top chicken with cilantro and serve.

makes 4 to 6 servings

INGREDIENTS

3 pounds skinless, bone-in chicken pieces
2 tablespoons extra-virgin olive oil
1 teaspoon salt
1 teaspoon cumin seeds
1 teaspoon nigella seeds (optional)
1 cup chicken stock
1 medium onion, sliced
3 saffron strands
1 teaspoon turmeric powder
1 tablespoon lemon zest
¼ cup lemon juice
12 black olives, pitted
2 tablespoons fresh cilantro, chopped

spicy chipotle chicken burrito

1. Place all ingredients, except tortillas, into the pressure cooker; secure lid.

2. Set pressure cooker to RICE and timer to 10 minutes.

3. When cooking is complete, assemble the burritos by spooning the chicken mixture down the center of each tortilla and rolling them into burritos.

Deb's Tip:
To make them even more delicious, serve the burritos with lettuce, avocado and sour cream.

makes 4 to 6 servings

INGREDIENTS

4 boneless, skinless chicken breasts, chopped into 1-inch pieces
1 cup chicken stock
2 whole chipotles in adobo sauce
1 teaspoon cumin seeds
1 teaspoon salt
1 teaspoon freshly ground pepper
1 teaspoon sugar
1 can (10 ounces) Mexican tomatoes with green chilies and lime
1 cup jasmine rice
1 cup black beans, cooked
½ cup cheddar cheese, shredded
2 tablespoons fresh cilantro, chopped
6 (12-inches each) flour tortillas

turkey pot roast

1. Pat the turkey breast dry using paper towels.

2. Rub turkey breast with salt, pepper and poultry seasoning.

3. Preheat oil in a large skillet over medium heat.

4. Gently place the turkey breast into the skillet; sear until all sides are golden brown.

5. Transfer the turkey breast to the pressure cooker.

6. Place the onions and mushrooms into the skillet; cook for 2 minutes.

7. Add the beer and stock to deglaze the skillet; scrape up all the little bits from the bottom of the skillet then transfer the skillet contents to the pressure cooker.

8. Add the tomato paste, celery and thyme to the pressure cooker; stir then secure lid.

9. Set pressure cooker to MEAT and timer to 45 minutes.

10. When cooking is complete, carefully remove the lid and add remaining ingredients to the pressure cooker; secure lid.

11. Set pressure cooker to VEGGIE and timer to 10 minutes.

12. When cooking is complete, remove the thyme sprigs and serve.

makes 4 to 6 servings

INGREDIENTS

1 (4 pound) boneless turkey breast, rinsed
½ teaspoon sea salt
½ teaspoon freshly ground pepper
½ teaspoon poultry seasoning
1 tablespoon extra-virgin olive oil
1 medium onion, quartered
¼ cup mushrooms, sliced

½ cup amber beer
½ cup chicken stock
1 tablespoon tomato paste
2 celery stalks, diced
2 sprigs fresh thyme
4 red bliss potatoes, halved
3 carrots, peeled, cut into 2-inch pieces

turkey ropa vieja

1. Place all ingredients into the pressure cooker; secure lid.

2. Set pressure cooker to MEAT and timer to 30 minutes.

3. When cooking is complete, remove the bay leaf.

4. Using two forks, pull apart the turkey and serve.

makes 4 to 6 servings

INGREDIENTS

2 pounds turkey breast fillets
1 medium onion, chopped
4 garlic cloves, minced
2 parsnips, peeled and chopped
2 celery stalks, chopped
1 cup chicken stock
6 roma tomatoes, diced
1 teaspoon salt
½ teaspoon freshly ground pepper
1 teaspoon capers
1 Serrano pepper, seeded and diced
1 teaspoon ground cumin
1 bay leaf

meat

french dip sandwich

1. Place all ingredients, except rolls, into the pressure cooker; secure lid.

2. Set pressure cooker to MEAT and timer to 50 minutes.

3. When cooking is complete, remove the thyme sprig.

4. Divide the meat slices between the French rolls.

5. Serve with a dish of the meat juice from the pressure cooker as a dipping sauce.

makes 4 servings

INGREDIENTS

1 (2 pound) bottom round roast, cut into 1-inch slices
1 cup beef stock
1 tablespoon Worcestershire sauce
1 garlic clove, sliced
1 large sweet onion, quartered
1 tablespoon grape jelly
½ teaspoon salt
½ teaspoon freshly ground pepper
1 sprig fresh thyme
4 French rolls, toasted

corned beef reuben

1. Place all ingredients, except bread, sauerkraut, cheese and dressing, into the pressure cooker; secure lid.

2. Set pressure cooker to MEAT and timer to 45 minutes.

3. Divide the sauerkraut between 4 bread slices then top each slice with 1 slice of cheese and 1/2 tablespoon of Thousand Island dressing.

4. When cooking is complete, divide the corned beef between the prepared slices and top each with another slice of bread.

5. Serve immediately.

makes 4 servings

INGREDIENTS

1 (2 pound) corned beef, sliced ½-inch thick
1 medium onion, quartered
2 garlic cloves
1 carrot, peeled
½ cup water
1 teaspoon mustard seeds
1 bay leaf
8 slices rye bread, toasted
1 cup sauerkraut, drained
4 Swiss cheese slices
2 tablespoons Thousand Island dressing, divided

beef short ribs

1. Place all ingredients, except jelly and tomato paste, into the pressure cooker; secure lid.

2. Set pressure cooker to MEAT and timer to 40 minutes.

3. When cooking is complete, add the jelly and tomato paste to the pressure cooker; stir then secure the lid.

4. Set pressure cooker to MEAT and timer to 20 minutes.

5. When cooking is complete, strain the pressure cooker contents through a sieve into a container; reserve the vegetables in a bowl.

6. Refrigerate the stock for 30 minutes.

7. Place the short ribs back into the pressure cooker.

8. Set pressure cooker to KEEP WARM.

9. Using a blender, purée the vegetables until smooth then place them back into the pressure cooker.

10. Remove the stock from the refrigerator, discard the hardened fat and pour it back into the pressure cooker.

11. Stir well and serve immediately.

makes 4 servings

INGREDIENTS

4 beef short ribs
1 cup beef stock
1 teaspoon salt
½ teaspoon freshly ground pepper
1 leek (white part only), split
2 carrots, peeled and cut into 2-inch slices
2 celery stalks, sliced

4 garlic cloves
1 shallot, halved
2 sprigs fresh thyme
1 tablespoon Worcestershire sauce
1 teaspoon soy sauce
1 tablespoon grape jelly
1 tablespoon tomato paste

italian pot roast

1. Preheat oil in a large skillet over medium heat.

2. Season the roast with salt and pepper.

3. Add the roast to the skillet and sear for 3 minutes on each side.

4. Transfer the roast to the pressure cooker.

5. Drain the fat from the skillet.

6. Add the wine and stock to deglaze the skillet; scrape up all the little bits from the bottom of the skillet then transfer the skillet contents to the pressure cooker.

7. Add the onions, garlic, bell peppers, garlic powder, Italian seasoning and bay leaf to the pressure cooker; secure lid.

8. Set pressure cooker to MEAT and timer to 60 minutes.

9. When cooking is complete, discard the bay leaf then add the pasta sauce to the pressure cooker; secure lid.

10. Set pressure cooker to RICE and timer to 6 minutes.

11. When cooking is complete, serve over your favorite pasta or polenta.

makes 4 to 6 servings

INGREDIENTS

2 tablespoons extra-virgin olive oil
1 (4 pound) chuck roast
1 teaspoon salt
½ teaspoon freshly ground pepper
¼ cup dry red wine
1 cup beef stock
1 medium onion, sliced

3 garlic cloves, sliced
1 bell pepper, diced
1 teaspoon garlic powder
1 teaspoon Italian herb seasoning
1 bay leaf
1 bottle (28 ounces) pasta sauce
Pasta or polenta, cooked

holiday brisket with root veggies

1. Preheat oil in a large sauté pan over medium-high heat.

2. Season the brisket with salt and pepper.

3. Add the brisket to the pan and brown for 3 minutes on each side.

4. Transfer the brisket to the pressure cooker and drain the grease from the sauté pan.

5. Add the wine to deglaze the pan; scrape up all the little bits from the bottom of the pan then transfer the pan contents to the pressure cooker.

6. Add the onions, thyme, allspice berries, bay leaf, stock and tomato paste to the pressure cooker; secure lid.

7. Set pressure cooker to MEAT and timer to 60 minutes.

8. When cooking is complete, discard the thyme sprig and bay leaf.

9. Add remaining ingredients to the pressure cooker; secure lid.

10. Set pressure cooker to VEGGIE and timer to 5 minutes.

11. When cooking is complete, cut the brisket against the grain and serve.

makes 4 to 6 servings

INGREDIENTS

2 tablespoons extra-virgin olive oil
1 (3 pound) first cut brisket
1 teaspoon salt
1 teaspoon freshly ground pepper
½ cup port wine
1 cup sweet onions, sliced
1 sprig fresh thyme

4 allspice berries
1 bay leaf
1 cup beef stock
1 tablespoon tomato paste
½ cup carrots, peeled and sliced
½ cup parsnip, peeled and sliced
½ cup celery root, peeled and diced

moroccan lamb shanks

1. Preheat oil in a large skillet over medium-high heat.

2. Season the lamb shanks with salt and pepper.

3. Add the lamb to the skillet and sear each shank on all sides until browned.

4. Transfer the lamb shanks to the pressure cooker.

5. Drain the fat from the skillet.

6. Add the red wine to deglaze the skillet; scrape up all the little bits from the bottom of the skillet then transfer the skillet contents to the pressure cooker.

7. Add remaining ingredients, except cilantro, to the pressure cooker; secure lid.

8. Set pressure cooker to MEAT and timer to 60 minutes.

9. When cooking is complete, top with cilantro and serve.

makes 4 servings

INGREDIENTS

2 tablespoons extra-virgin olive oil
4 (1 pound each) lamb shanks
½ teaspoon salt
½ teaspoon freshly ground pepper
½ cup dry red wine
½ cup chicken stock
2 tablespoons tomato paste
½ cup carrots, diced
1 shallot, minced
3 garlic cloves, minced
½ teaspoon cumin seeds
½ teaspoon coriander seeds
½ teaspoon pumpkin pie spice
1 can (16.5 ounces) petite diced tomatoes
2 tablespoons fresh cilantro, chopped

asian style baby back ribs

1. Place all ingredients, except brown sugar, into the pressure cooker; secure lid.

2. Set pressure cooker to MEAT and timer to 25 minutes.

3. When cooking is complete, transfer the ribs to a broiler pan, bone-side down.

4. Preheat the broiler on high.

5. To reduce the liquid in the pressure cooker, set to RICE and timer to 10 minutes; let cook with the lid off until the liquid turns into a syrup-like glaze.

6. While the liquid is reducing, rub the meat side of the ribs with brown sugar and place the ribs under the broiler for 10 minutes or until golden brown.

7. Pour some glaze over the ribs and serve with glaze on the side.

Deb's Tip:
If you don't have fresh ginger, the bottled variety commonly found in the sushi section of your supermarket is a perfect substitute.

makes 2 to 4 servings

INGREDIENTS

1 full slab baby back ribs
½ cup chicken stock
2 tablespoons fresh ginger, sliced
1 medium onion, quartered
2 garlic cloves
2 tablespoons sesame oil
2 tablespoons soy sauce
2 tablespoons rice wine vinegar
2 tablespoons brown sugar

pork chops l'orange

1. Preheat a large skillet over medium-high heat.

2. Rub the pork chops with olive oil then season with salt.

3. Place the pork chops into the skillet and sear for 2 minutes on each side.

4. Transfer the pork chops to the pressure cooker.

5. Add the chicken stock to deglaze the skillet; scrape up all the little bits from the bottom of the skillet then transfer the skillet contents to the pressure cooker.

6. Add remaining ingredients to the pressure cooker; secure lid.

7. Set pressure cooker to MEAT and timer to 20 minutes.

8. When cooking is complete, serve immediately.

makes 4 servings

INGREDIENTS

4 bone-in pork chops, 1-inch thick
1 tablespoon extra-virgin olive oil
½ teaspoon salt
½ cup chicken stock
¼ cup brown sugar
1 teaspoon cider vinegar
1 teaspoon freshly grated ginger
½ teaspoon dry mustard
1 teaspoon dried marjoram
1 teaspoon orange zest
1 sprig fresh thyme
½ teaspoon black pepper
2 oranges, peeled and sectioned

desserts

poached pears

1. Pour the wine into the pressure cooker.

2. Using a melon baller, core the bottom of each pear.

3. Cut off the bottom of each pear so they sit flat.

4. Place the pears into the pressure cooker.

5. Add the rosemary and peppercorns to the pressure cooker; secure lid.

6. Set pressure cooker to VEGGIE and timer to 10 minutes.

7. When cooking is complete, transfer the pears to a platter.

8. To reduce the liquid inside the pressure cooker, set pressure cooker to RICE and timer to 10 minutes; cook with the lid off until the liquid turns into a syrup.

9. Top the pears with syrup and serve.

Deb's Tip:
Serve the poached pears topped with your favorite ice cream.

makes 4 servings

INGREDIENTS

1 bottle (750ml) port wine
4 Bartlett pears, peeled
3 sprigs rosemary
½ teaspoon whole peppercorns

lemon curd

1. Process the sugar in a blender until very fine then transfer it to a 2-quart bowl.

2. Add remaining ingredients, except water, to the bowl; beat using a whisk.

3. Cover the bowl tightly in aluminum foil.

4. Pour the water into the pressure cooker.

5. Place the bowl into the pressure cooker; secure lid.

6. Set pressure cooker to RICE and timer to 13 minutes.

7. When cooking is complete, carefully remove the foil then whisk the ingredients well.

8. Refrigerate for 1 hour before serving.

makes 4 servings

INGREDIENTS

1¼ cups sugar
2 tablespoons lemon zest
½ cup bottled lemon juice
⅓ cup unsalted butter, cut into small pieces
4 egg yolks
3 large eggs
1 cup water

gluten-free banana bread

1. In a food processor fitted with a metal S blade, combine the bananas, butter and nectar; process for 1 minute or until smooth.

2. Add the extract, apricots, zest, almonds and flax seeds to the food processor; process for 1 minute.

3. While processing, add the eggs (1 at a time) through the feed tube and process until smooth.

4. Remove the blade from the food processor then add remaining ingredients; stir to incorporate but do not overmix.

5. Apply non-stick spray to the pressure cooker.

6. Pour the batter into the pressure cooker; secure lid.

7. Set pressure cooker to RICE and timer to 20 minutes.

8. When cooking is complete, invert onto a serving platter and serve hot or cold.

makes 6 to 8 servings

INGREDIENTS

3 ripe bananas
⅓ cup unsalted butter
¾ cup agave nectar
1 teaspoon banana extract
1 cup dried apricots
1 teaspoon orange zest
½ cup blanched almonds
¼ cup flax seeds
2 large eggs
1¾ cups gluten-free baking mix
1 teaspoon xanthan gum
2 teaspoons baking powder
½ teaspoon salt
½ teaspoon ground cinnamon

chocolate cherry cordial bread pudding

1. In a large bowl, soak the cherries in brandy for 5 minutes.

2. Add remaining ingredients to the bowl; mix well.

3. Apply non-stick spray to the pressure cooker.

4. Transfer the bowl contents to the pressure cooker; secure lid.

5. Set pressure cooker to RICE and timer to 15 minutes.

6. When cooking is complete, serve hot or cold.

Deb's Tip:
If you don't have brandy, just use water.

makes 6 to 8 servings

INGREDIENTS

6 ounces dried cherries
2 tablespoons brandy
4 large eggs, beaten
1½ cups cream
½ cup brown sugar
1 teaspoon vanilla extract
1 cup chocolate chips
1 loaf challah bread, cubed and toasted

crème caramel

1. In a microwave-safe container, combine caramel ingredients; stir.

2. Microwave on high for about 3 minutes or until mixture turns into a light golden color (cooking times may vary depending on your microwave).

3. Divide the caramel between four ½-cup glass ramekins; tilt the ramekins to distribute the caramel evenly across the bottoms then let cool for 5 minutes.

4. In a bowl, combine custard ingredients; beat until well combined without creating too much foam.

5. Divide the custard between the ramekins.

6. Wrap each ramekin tightly in aluminum foil.

7. Pour 1 cup of water into the pressure cooker.

8. Stack the ramekins inside the pressure cooker; secure lid.

9. Set pressure cooker to VEGGIE and timer to 5 minutes.

10. When cooking is complete, remove the ramekins from the pressure cooker, let rest for 30 minutes at room temperature then chill for 1 hour.

11. Remove the foil, run a sharp knife around the edges of the ramekins, invert onto a plate and serve.

makes 4 servings

CARAMEL INGREDIENTS	CUSTARD INGREDIENTS
½ cup granulated sugar 1 tablespoon corn syrup 1 tablespoon water	½ cup granulated sugar 1 tablespoon corn syrup 1 tablespoon water

chocolate pots de crème

1. Apply non-stick spray to four ½-cup ramekins; set aside.

2. Place the chocolate into a mixing bowl.

3. Pour the cream and milk into a saucepan over medium heat.

4. When the cream begins to simmer, pour it into the chocolate bowl; stir until smooth.

5. In a separate bowl, combine remaining ingredients, except water.

6. Slowly pour the chocolate mixture into the yolk mixture; mix well then divide the mixture between the ramekins.

7. Wrap each ramekin in aluminum foil.

8. Pour the water into the pressure cooker and stack the ramekins inside the pressure cooker; secure lid.

9. Set pressure cooker to VEGGIE and timer to 10 minutes.

10. When cooking is complete, remove the ramekins and let rest at room temperature for 30 minutes.

11. Remove the foil and serve.

Deb's Tip:
You can also serve this dessert chilled, topped with whipped cream.

makes 4 servings

INGREDIENTS

2 ounces bittersweet chocolate, finely chopped
1 cup heavy cream
1 cup whole milk
4 egg yolks
2 tablespoons sugar
½ teaspoon orange zest
⅛ teaspoon salt
1 cup water

blood orange pots de crème

1. In a bowl, combine egg, yolks and sugar; beat for 30 seconds using a fork.

2. Add the heavy cream, juices and zest to the bowl; whisk until the sugar is dissolved.

3. Strain the custard through a sieve.

4. Divide the custard between four ½-cup ramekins.

5. Wrap the ramekins tightly in aluminum foil.

6. Pour the water into the pressure cooker.

7. Place the ramekins into the pressure cooker; secure lid.

8. Set pressure cooker to VEGGIE and timer to 5 minutes.

9. When cooking is complete, remove the foil and chill for at least 30 minutes before serving.

makes 4 servings

INGREDIENTS

1 large egg
4 egg yolks
¼ cup sugar
1 cup heavy cream
½ cup blood orange juice
1 teaspoon lemon juice
1 teaspoon lemon zest
1 cup water

orange upside down cake

1. Place the butter into the pressure cooker.

2. Set pressure cooker to RICE and let butter melt with the lid off.

3. Add the brown sugar and syrup to the pressure cooker; stir until smooth.

4. Turn off the pressure cooker then top the sugar mixture with layers of orange rings.

5. In a large bowl, combine flour, sugar, baking powder, baking soda, cinnamon and allspice; mix well.

6. In a separate bowl, combine oil, carrots, applesauce and vanilla; mix well.

7. Add the carrot mixture to the flour mixture and mix using a spatula; add remaining ingredients and mix well.

8. Apply non-stick spray to the pressure cooker.

9. Pour the batter evenly into the pressure cooker over the orange slices; secure lid.

10. Set pressure cooker to RICE and timer to 30 minutes.

11. When cooking is complete, remove the lid and let the cake rest for 20 minutes inside the pressure cooker.

12. Invert the cake onto a cake stand and serve.

makes 6 servings

INGREDIENTS

2 tablespoons unsalted butter
2 tablespoons brown sugar
1 teaspoon maple syrup
1 large orange, sliced into thin rings
1½ cups unbleached all purpose flour
1 cup sugar
1 teaspoon baking powder
1 teaspoon baking soda

1 teaspoon ground cinnamon
½ teaspoon allspice
½ cup safflower oil
1 cup carrots, shredded
1 cup applesauce
1 teaspoon vanilla extract
½ cup raisins
¼ cup chopped pecans (optional)

white chocolate cheesecake

1. Preheat oven to 350 degrees; place cookies, almonds and butter into a food processor fitted with the metal S blade then secure the lid.

2. Pulse for 1 minute or until an even crumb is achieved.

3. Place a sheet of parchment paper over the base of a 7-inch springform pan; secure the ring around the pan then apply non-stick spray to the inside of the pan.

4. Press the cookie mixture into the bottom of the pan and bake for 10 minutes; let cool.

5. In a small saucepan over medium heat, bring the cream to a simmer then remove from heat; add the chocolate to the cream and stir until smooth.

6. In a mixer or food processor, combine the cream cheese and sugar; mix until very smooth.

7. While mixing, add the eggs (one at a time) through the feed tube then add the lemon juice, vanilla and white chocolate mixture; mix until smooth then transfer mixture to the cooled springform pan.

8. Wrap the pan tightly in aluminum foil; pour the water into the pressure cooker then place the pan into the pressure cooker and secure the lid.

9. Set pressure cooker to MEAT and timer to 40 minutes.

10. When cooking is complete and pressure is released from the pressure cooker, carefully remove the pan from the pressure cooker.

11. Let rest at room temperature for 30 minutes then refrigerate for 3 hours before serving.

makes 8 servings

INGREDIENTS

8 vanilla cream cookies
¼ cup almonds, slivered
1 tablespoon unsalted butter
¼ cup heavy cream
8 ounces white chocolate, finely chopped
12 ounces cream cheese

¼ cup sugar
2 large eggs
1 teaspoon lemon juice
1 teaspoon vanilla extract
1 cup water

mint chocolate cheesecake

1. Preheat the oven to 350 degrees; place a sheet of parchment paper over the base of a 7-inch springform pan, secure the ring around the pan then apply non-stick spray to the inside of the pan.

2. Place the crust ingredients into a food processor and process until smooth; press the mixture into the base of the springform pan and bake for 10 minutes.

3. In a microwave-safe bowl, microwave the chocolate morsels for the filling at 50% power for 1 minute; stir and microwave for an additional 30 seconds.

4. In the food processor, combine the cream cheese and sugar; process until smooth then add remaining filling ingredients to the food processor; mix well then add the melted chocolate to the food processor and process until smooth.

5. Pour the filling into the springform pan and wrap it tightly in aluminum foil.

6. Pour 1 cup of water into the pressure cooker then place the pan into the pressure cooker; secure lid.

7. Set pressure cooker to MEAT and timer to 40 minutes.

8. When cooking is complete, remove the pan from the pressure cooker and let cool at room temperature.

9. To make the fudge topping, in a saucepan over medium heat, bring the cream to a boil; remove from heat, add the chocolate to the saucepan, stir until smooth then add the mint extract.

10. Pour the fudge topping over the cheesecake, cover in plastic wrap and refrigerate for 2 hours before serving.

makes 4 servings

CRUST INGREDIENTS

14 thin mint chocolate cookies
2 tablespoons unsalted butter

FUDGE TOPPING INGREDIENTS

½ cup heavy cream
1 cup semi-sweet chocolate morsels
½ teaspoon mint extract

FILLING INGREDIENTS

1½ cups semi-sweet chocolate morsels
2 packages (8 ounces each) cream cheese
½ cup sugar
1 tablespoon all purpose flour
2 large eggs
1 teaspoon mint extract
1 teaspoon vanilla extract

key lime cheesecake

1. Preheat oven to 350 degrees; place a sheet of parchment paper over the base of a 7-inch springform pan.

2. Secure the ring around the springform pan; apply non-stick spray to the pan.

3. Place all crust ingredients into a food processor; process for 30 seconds or until fine crumbs are achieved then press the mixture firmly into the base of the pan.

4. Place the pan into the oven and bake for 10 minutes.

5. Place the cream cheese and milk into the food processor; process for 1 minute or until very smooth; while processing, add the eggs (one at a time) through the feed tube then continue to process for 30 seconds.

6. Add remaining filling ingredients then process for an additional 30 seconds.

7. Pour filling into the baked crust then wrap the entire springform pan in aluminum foil.

8. Pour 1 cup of water into the pressure cooker then place the pan into the pressure cooker; secure lid.

9. Set pressure cooker to MEAT and timer to 40 minutes.

10. When cooking is complete, remove the pan from the pressure cooker and let rest at room temperature for 30 minutes.

11. Refrigerate the covered cheesecake for 2 hours before serving.

makes 6 to 8 servings

CRUST INGREDIENTS

10 vanilla crème wafers
2 tablespoons unsalted butter
¼ cup macadamia nuts

FILLING INGREDIENTS

3 packages (8 ounces each) cream cheese
1 can (14 ounces) sweetened condensed milk
3 large eggs
1 tablespoon all purpose flour
⅓ cup key lime juice
1 teaspoon lime zest
1 teaspoon butter nut extract
2 drops green food coloring (optional)

index

a

artichokes in lemon dill 67

asian style baby back ribs 116

b

baby beets & carrots 68

barbeque chicken 89

beef bourguignon 44

beef short ribs 108

beet greens smoked turkey wings 70

black eyed pea burger 80

blood orange pots de crème 132

brussels sprouts w/ pearl onions 74

buffalo chicken mac & cheese 62

c

chicken & dumpling soup 34

chicken soup 30

chicken with sweet potato dumplings 90

chocolate pots de crème 130

classic beef stew 42

corned beef reuben 106

creamy quinoa pudding 56

creamy spinach mashed potatoes 50

crème caramel 128

cheesecakes

key lime cheesecake 140

mint chocolate cheesecake 138

white chocolate cheesecake 136

chicken

barbeque chicken 89

buffalo chicken mac & cheese 62

chicken & dumpling soup 34

chicken soup 30

chicken with sweet potato dumplings 90

easy chicken curry 92

greek lemon chicken soup 32

moroccan chicken 96

rich chicken stock 28

spicy chipotle chicken burrito 98

thai chicken curry 94

chocolate

chocolate pots de crème 130

mint chocolate cheesecake 138

white chocolate cheesecake 136

chocolate cherry bread pudding 126

desserts

blood orange pots de crème 132

chocolate cherry bread pudding 12

chocolate pots de crème 130

crème caramel 128

gluten-free banana bread 124

key lime cheesecake 140

lemon curd 122

mint chocolate cheesecake 138

orange upside down cake 134

poached pears 121

white chocolate cheesecake 136

e

easy chicken curry 92

f

french dip sandwich 105

fresh vegetable soup 9

g

greek lemon chicken soup 32

gluten-free banana bread 124

gluten-free

gluten-free banana bread 124

...ains

...eamy quinoa pudding 56

...inoa turkey meatloaf 58

...isfleisch 64

...icy bulgur pilaf 54

...el cut oats 47

...heat berry salad 48

...ild rice cranberries & pecan stuffing 52

...day brisket with root veggies 112

...sour noodle soup with shrimp 14

...an pot roast 110

...ocha squash soup 12

... lime cheesecake 140

...on curd 122

...on dill green beans 72

...tils with italian turkey sausage 24

... country boil 26

...mb

...oroccan lamb shanks 114

m

martin's lobster asparagus soup 18

mint chocolate cheesecake 138

moroccan chicken 96

moroccan lamb shanks 114

meat

beef bourguignon 44

beef short ribs 108

classic beef stew 42

corned beef reuben 106

french dip sandwich 105

holiday brisket with root veggies 112

italian pot roast 110

o

orange upside down cake 134

p

parsnip purée with shallots 78

pizza soup 22

poached pears 121

pork & apple stew 38

pork chops l'orange 118

potato leek soup 20

pasta

buffalo chicken mac & cheese 62

pork

asian style baby back ribs 116

pork & apple stew 38

pork chops l'orange 118

potatoes

chicken with sweet potato dumplings 90

creamy spinach mashed potatoes 50

potato leek soup 20

wolf's warm potato salad 82

q

quinoa turkey meatloaf 58

r

reisfleisch 64

rich beef stock 40

rich chicken stock 28

s

shrimp bisque 16

spicy bulgur pilaf 54

spicy chipotle chicken burrito 98

steel cut oats 47

stuffed onions 76

stuffed turkey peppers with couscous 60

swiss chard white bean stew 36

szechuan veggies 84

salad

wheat berry salad 48

sandwiches

corned beef reuben 106

french dip sandwich 105

shrimp

hot sour noodle soup with shrimp 14

low country boil 26

shrimp bisque 16

soups

chicken & dumpling soup 34

chicken soup 30

fresh vegetable soup 9

greek lemon chicken soup 32

hot sour noodle soup with shrimp 14

kabocha squash soup 12

martin's lobster asparagus soup 18

pizza soup 22

potato leek soup 20

shrimp bisque 16

tomato florentine 10

stews

classic beef stew 42

lentils with italian turkey sausage 24

low country boil 26

pork & apple stew 38

swiss chard white bean stew 36

stocks

rich beef stock 40

rich chicken stock 28

t

thai chicken curry 94

tomato florentine 10

turkey pot roast 100

turkey ropa vieja 102

turkey

beet greens w/ smoked turkey wings 70

lentils with italian turkey sausage 24

quinoa turkey meatloaf 58

stuffed turkey peppers with couscous 60

turkey pot roast 100

turkey ropa vieja 102

v

vegetable curry 86

vegetables

artichokes in lemon dill 67

baby beets & carrots 68

beet greens w/ smoked turkey wings

black eyed pea burger 80

brussels sprouts with pearl onions 74

creamy spinach mashed potatoes 50

lemon dill green beans 72

parsnip purée with shallots 78

stuffed onions 76

stuffed turkey peppers with couscous

szechuan veggies 84

vegetable curry 86

wolf's warm potato salad 82

w

wheat berry salad 48

white chocolate cheesecake 136

wild rice cranberries & pecan stuffing 5

wolf's warm potato salad 82

For more of Deb's delicious ideas, please visit:
www.cookingwithdeb.com